The Waiting Season

A BOOK FOR SINGLES IN THE WAIT

Queenie Patton

Copyright © 2024 by Queenie Patton

All rights reserved. No part of this publication may be reproduced, distributed or transmitted in any form or by any means, including photocopying, recording, or other electronic or mechanical methods, without the prior written permission of the publisher, except in the case of brief quotations embodied in critical reviews and certain other noncommercial uses permitted by copyright law. For mission requests, write to the publisher, addressed " Attention: Permissions Coordinator," at the address below.

Queenie Patton/Rejoice Essential Publishing
PO BOX 512
Effingham, SC 29541
www.republishing.org

Author's Contact: queauntris@yahoo.com

Unless otherwise indicated, scripture is taken from the King James Version.

Scripture quotations marked (NLT) are taken from the Holy Bible, New Living Translation, copyright ©1996, 2004, 2015 by Tyndale House Foundation. Used by permission of Tyndale House Publishers, Carol Stream, Illinois 60188. All rights reserved.

Scripture quotations marked (CEB) are taken from the COMMON ENGLISH BIBLE. © Copyright 2011 COMMON ENGLISH BIBLE. All rights reserved. Used by permission. (www.CommonEnglishBible.com).

Scripture quotations marked (AMP) are taken from the Amplified Bible, Copyright © 2015 by The Lockman Foundation. Used by permission.

Scripture quotations marked MSG are taken from The Message, copyright © 1993, 2002, 2018 by Eugene H. Peterson. Used by permission of NavPress. All rights reserved. Represented by Tyndale House Publishers.

The Waiting Season/Queenie Patton

ISBN-13: 979-8-3305-2114-2

Acknowledgements

MAMA, THANK YOU SO much for giving me life and always supporting me in everything I do. I thank you for training me up as a child in church. Without you and Granny, I wouldn't be the woman I am today.

I'm grateful for my Daddy Charles who is no longer with me. We had a moment, but God restored what we lost.

To my sisters and brother in love, thank you for loving me the way that I am and always supporting my Shenanigans as your older sister.

Acknowledgements

To my nieces and nephews, who bring so much joy to our family, know that Auntie loves you so much.

To my Auntie, thank you so much for getting me in trouble (insider) at an early age. Thanks for being apart of the village.

To my family and village, thank you for caring for the younger me. Where the foundation was broken, you helped rebuild it and cultivate the wiser woman that God has destined for me to be.

To my friends, thank you for your encouragement and prayers along the way and for accepting me for who I am. Thank you for always keeping it real with me and not sugar-coating anything.

To my home church, thanks for planting the seed and pushing me when I didn't want to.

Also, thank you for showing me how to be an effective leader.

Pastor, Apostle Sam and Dr. Rico, thanks for always teaching and preaching the word of God and pouring into me. To not only be a hearer of the word, but a doer of the word. I appreciate you both from the bottom of my heart. This wouldn't be possible without you two.

Table of Contents

FOREWORD..viii
INTRODUCTION..1
CHAPTER 1: Why Are You Single?....................4
CHAPTER 2: Healing is Necessary..................10
CHAPTER 3: Done Recovering.......................16
CHAPTER 4: Patience in the Wait..................22
CHAPTER 5: Let the Father Lead You.............26
CHAPTER 6: Enjoy the Years of Your
                          Singleness....................................31
ABOUT THE AUTHOR...39

Foreword

WHY DO FOOLS FALL in love? If you've ever seen that movie, you know that it's a bunch of foolishness around there. But what happens when the foolish become unfoolish and wait on the Lord?

I felt truly honored and joyful when Queenie asked me to pen this foreword. As she unveils her heartfelt book on the journey of being single and waiting for the right man to become her husband, she has written a wonderful book of instructions for other single ladies.

For over 20 years, Queenie and I have navigated the ups and downs of life together, sharing countless laughs, dreams, and adventures. I fondly remember our first flight together, a leap into the unknown that set the tone for many more exhilarating experiences we would share. I was terrified to fly, but she held my hand and said, "It's going to be ok, friend." Queenie has been a steadfast supporter through every business venture and personal challenge. Her unwavering loyalty and consistent presence in my life have been a source of strength and inspiration.

Dedicated to her family and her faith, Queenie possesses a beautiful anointing that shines through in her writing. She has a unique ability to connect with others, and I have no doubt that her powerful message will resonate deeply with women who are patiently waiting for their own Mr. Right. Queenie's insights, wisdom, and authenticity will guide and uplift those on similar journeys, reminding them that their stories are valuable and their patience is worthwhile.

I am incredibly proud of Queenie for pouring her heart into this book. Her bold and courageous spirit to share her experiences and wisdom is a gift to us all. As she writes about waiting with hope and purpose, I am reminded of the beautiful verse from *Psalm 27:14:* *"Wait for the*

Lord; be strong, and let your heart take courage; wait for the Lord!" This verse encapsulates the essence of her message and encourages us all to trust in God's perfect timing.

So, to every woman who picks up this book, prepare to be inspired and empowered. Through this book, be reminded that your wait is not in vain; love will find you in the perfect time. God's perfect time.

With all my love and admiration,

Shantina Rochelle Sandifer

***

I know what you may be thinking. Here is another book for singles telling you what to do while waiting. You're probably thinking, "What can I learn from this? I've been hearing the same thing for years and still have the same relationship status as single." You may be in a season where you are just frustrated and feel like giving up on love. You may feel like God has forgotten about you and came to the resolve that marriage is not in your future. You may be in a season where you feel like all your friends and everyone around you are getting married, and you're petitioning God when it will finally be your turn. If you feel this way, you are not alone, and I have good news for you. This book will help equip you with what you need to help you navigate in your single season. It will help restore your faith and hope and rebuild your trust in God. You will no longer see being single as a curse but a blessing. The enemy's main goal is to get you discouraged so you can lose faith in God and what He has promised. Your relationship status does not define you; you are defined by who God has called you to be. You're the head and not the tail. You are above and not beneath.

As you read each page, this book will help unravel some things from your past, unhealed trauma, and areas of unforgiveness, and help bring forth healing from rejection. It will change your life trajectory and give you a new perspective on singleness and how it looks as you wait on God for your spouse. *The Waiting Season* by Queenie is unlike any other book you may have read, and it is for men and women. This manuscript will leave you feeling encouraged, valued, seen, heard, inspired, and empowered. Queenie is new to the writing world and is a first-time author. I have known Queenie for over 22 years and always knew she had a story to tell. She has always been a social butterfly, family-oriented, and has a great love for people. She is a kingdom woman, a servant, a leader, and has a passion for uplifting singles, both men and women. In this manuscript, you will find that she is very transparent, has stepped outside her comfort zone, and has poured her heart out. As you journey through the pages, may you experience healing, be encouraged, and have a newfound hope in Christ.

Be blessed
Antionette Williams

Introduction

*T*HOUGHTS FROM QUEENIE

Hello Everyone,

In 2018, God gave me the vision to write this book, but I was thinking it was just a thought and not God speaking to me. *James 1:8 NLT says, "Their loyalty is divided between God and the world, and they are unstable in everything they do."* I was so double-minded in my thoughts to the point I was like, "Nope, I can't do this."

In 2022, the Lord spoke to me about writing and God placed this book back in my spirit to write for singles. I was still asking the Lord, "What am I going to say? I'm not equipped enough for this journey," but the Lord God says, "I AM." I feel like singles are given such a bad stigma because we are still single after so many years. There's nothing wrong with singleness. It gives you the opportunity and to be better for your self and your future spouse if you desire to be married to grow your relationship with Christ. You get to explore life with no limits, pursue your dreams, and become the man or woman that God called you to be.

Some of us have attracted the wrong person for years, me included. During my reflection from 2018 to now, the Lord showed me why I attracted the wrong person. I felt like I had to look, act, say, or become someone to attract this person because that is what I saw or was told. I did this for years, only to find out it was me. I had to heal from childhood daddy issues that I never healed from until recently. After my healing journey, God spoke to me during a fast in September 2023 that I have restored the years the locust have hath eaten (Joel 2:25).

Please know that I'm on this journey with you. I'm just a vessel, the Lord has the pen. I'm not here to tell you how to date or who to choose. My prayers are that this book can be-

Introduction

gin to remove the stigma behind singleness, that you're not easily distracted by what you see in the world, that you seek the Lord God (Matthew 6:33), that you live in the fullness of God, and that you enjoy the years of singleness until God presents your spouse. At any moment, if you feel like you are going back to your old ways, I want you to pick up this book to remind you that your wait is not in vain.

CHAPTER 1

Why Are You Single?

I KNOW YOU ARE TIRED of hearing the phrase, "Why are you still single?" Can I be transparent? Half of us could have been married by now to the wrong person or in a marriage where we would be so unhappy with that person. I do believe the Lord shielded us from people who were no good for us. I look at rejection now as God's protection. The Lord is protecting us when we don't even realize it.

So, why not be single until the woman or man that the Lord God has for you comes along? Singleness is not a CURSE; I repeat, it's not a CURSE. It's just a Season! Now, I can't tell you how long that season will be, but trust Him in the wait.

In our singleness, we can live a life pleasing to the Lord and not be concerned for someone else at the moment. Singleness gives you the opportunity to know who you are and WHOSES YOU are in Christ Jesus! Also, if you don't know, seek the Lord for what your purpose is in life. The Bible says in *Matthew 7:7-8*, *"Ask, and it will be given to you; seek, and you will find; knock, and the door will be opened to you. For everyone who asks receives, and he who seeks finds, and to him who knocks it will be opened."* Find out what your gifts and talents are in the Lord. Grow with the Lord in this season and get yourself in a Bible based church where they teach the Gospel of Jesus Christ. God will give you all the directions and guidance you need.

I know you may not want to hear this but there is so much freedom with the Father, so much freedom! When you get to the place where there is freedom in the Lord, loneliness will no longer take over. Let the Lord God fill that void. I promise that you will no longer be the same.

The Waiting Season

Can I be honest? I haven't always been this way, but in 2022, my life shifted and I told the Lord I would not continue to move this way. I saw life differently after losing a parent unexpectedly. We can leave this life at any moment and I want to hear "Well done my good and faithful servant." I sought the Lord after my dad's death and my life immediately shifted. My prayer is, if you don't know Jesus, get to know Him and accept Him as Lord and Savior. God can give you the desires of your heart (Psalm 37:4), but you have to let him in.

Let's pray.

Lord God, I thank you for my singleness. I know that it's only temporary and you can move at any time with my spouse. In my waiting season help me to work on myself to be a better person for you and my future spouse. Use me for your purpose. Help me, Lord God, to die to my flesh daily and make you the apple of my eye. In Jesus' name. Amen!

Why Are You Single?

JOURNAL

1. What are some things you can work on to become a better you?
2. Do you know your purpose? Pray and seek the Lord for it. When it's revealed, write it down.

_____

_____

_____

_____

_____

_____

_____

_____

_____

_____

_____

_____

_____

_____

The Waiting Season

Why Are You Single?

CHAPTER 2

Healing Is Necessary

It's very important that we heal before we start dating. We feel like sometimes the person that we are in a relationship/courtship with can help us through our healing journey process. They can't heal you. Only Jesus can do the healing. One of the scriptures I kept reading in 2022 was, *"The Lord is close to the brokenhearted and saves those who are crushed in spirit (Psalms 34:18)."* The Lord God is so near to us when we are going through, but we have to lay our burdens at His feet. We have to do the work for our healing. If not, we will begin to bleed on others, which in turn can hurt them or cause them to hurt you.

When dating, you don't want to run into a shark. Just like a shark can smell blood, a person not sent by God can too. A person can tell when someone is vulnerable and can begin to pick at that wound until you are torn down, but God is not like that. He wants to take that wound and begin to reconstruct the wound to where it's no longer an open wound which is now healed. Healing is necessary if we want what God has for us in a spouse.

We like to point the blame at the other person at times when we are the issue. Some of us go into a relationship broken and in turn damaging them because they are not living up to what we want. We can't make them become who we want them to be. They have to do their own work.

Some traumas in our lives are so deeply rooted, but we don't know how deep they are until we start dating. I know for me, I didn't start to notice until after I started therapy and had to apologize to an ex because I was looking for him to fill a void because of my daddy issues. I believe once we identify our traumas and where they are coming from, we can date a lot differently. You will begin to identify those familiar spirits that you were attracted to when you were broken.

We have to do the work and if you have to go to therapy, then go. Healing is not fun, but it's necessary for your future and future spouse. GO GET HEALED! DO THE WORK! Be intentional about your future.

Let's Pray.

Lord God, help me to heal from my open wounds and make me stronger. Help me not to put my old traumas on my future spouse. Clean me Lord from the inside out. Make me whole in you. In Jesus' name, Amen!

JOURNAL

Ask yourself these questions.
1. Have you noticed a pattern in the people you are dating?
2. Ask yourself why do you keep attracting familiar spirits?

Healing Is Necessary

Take a moment to write down the patterns you see in dating and seek the Lord on it. It could be some fleshy things that you have to die to so you don't keep attracting the same person in a different body.

_____

_____

_____

_____

_____

_____

_____

_____

_____

_____

_____

_____

_____

_____

_____

_____

The Waiting Season

Healing Is Necessary

CHAPTER 3

Done Recovering

WHY DO WE KEEP recovering over situations that God already told us no too? I clearly heard the Lord say no to me once, but I did it anyway. I felt like I could handle the consequences on my own. Then I realized I couldn't handle it. I would get upset because I gave myself to this person who wasn't for me, over and over again. It was exhausting and I needed the Lord to pick me back up and make me new again, but if I had listened to Him the first time I wouldn't have needed to recover.

One of my favorite scriptures are *Proverbs 3:5-6*, *"Trust in the Lord with all your heart and lean not into your own understanding, in all your ways acknowledge him and he will direct your path."* I have quoted these scripture for years, but didn't trust Him to do so. For years, I would remove Him because I felt like He never heard me. I was like, "Lord God where are you? Why am I making the same mistakes over and over?" When I didn't hear Him, I moved according to my will and not His will. When I did that, I was in relationships and situationships that broke me repeatedly. When you are broken, brokenness attracts the wrong people. When you attract the wrong person, you will continue to add scars and wounds that God never intended for you to have.

What I found out during my healing journey is that some issues are deeply rooted and we have to heal from them first before we let someone else in our lives. We need to stop recovering from the same relationships over and over that have caused us heartache and confusion. Know that God is not the author of confusion, but of peace (1 Corinthians 14:33). So, if it's confusion, it's not of God. Take a moment to examine why you keep attracting the same person that's not good for you over and over. Let's stop recovering and live in the fullness and peace of God.

Get an accountability partner or partners who can go to war in the spirit for you when you are weak in your flesh. I remember praying for mine, and the Lord reminded me that I already had them because iron sharpens iron, so one person sharpens another (Proverbs 27:17 NIV).

The thief comes to steal, kill, and destroy, but I have come that they may have life and have it abundantly (John 10:10). God wants the very best for you, so stop recovering from that person that brought you heartache the first time! Say it out LOUD, "I am DONE RECOVERING!"

Let's pray!

God, give me the wisdom and discernment to choose wisely. Help me to know that my body is a temple of God and if I wait according to your word, I don't have to keep recovering from people who are no good for me. Love starts with me so help me to love myself first like you love me, because no one can love me the right way if I'm still broken.

In Jesus' name, Amen!

JOURNAL

Let's stop recovering and start living. If they don't bring you peace, they are not for you. Write down people or circumstances that you are done recovering from. Write them down and take ACTION! Let's walk in the overflow of God's goodness.

_____

_____

_____

_____

_____

_____

_____

_____

_____

_____

The Waiting Season

Done Recovering

CHAPTER 4

Patience In The Wait

*S*INGLENESS DOES TEST YOUR patience. There have been many times when I have questioned the Lord, asking, "What's the hold up? Where is my husband?" I've even tried to make relationships happen that I knew had an expiration date. Over the past two years, I've have learned the waiting humbles you and makes you stronger.

I'm reminded of *James 1:3-4 AMP, "Be assured that the testing of your faith (through experience) produces endurance (leading a spiritual maturity, and inner peace), And let endurance have it's perfect result and do a thorough work, so that you may be perfect and completely developed (in your faith) lacking nothing."*

I always keep the story of Job at the front of my mind when I'm tested. He was tested heavily. God told the devil to test Job and I promise you, he won't budge. Job lost it ALL, but his faith never wavered. In the end, he received everything he lost back. We have to be like Job, regardless of the test that comes our way during life's journey because the reward would be greater.

I remember a sermon from my Pastor in which he stated that manifestation is based on the person and their obedience. That means you have to stay obedient to God's word and don't give up in the wait. I know it is easier said than done, but I've been there. I hardened my heart to the Lord for many years because things weren't happening the way I wanted them to, but I had to repent and ask the Lord for forgiveness. I had to totally give up my will for His will. That was the best thing I could have done. The Lord God has answered many of my prayers since I gave Him my yes.

Hannah was another person in the Bible who had to wait for the Lord to fulfill her desire to have a child. She waited years for a child, she prayed year after year for the Lord to help her conceive. She didn't faint on the Lord even though at times she felt like the Lord wasn't hearing her prayer, but she stayed at his feet until Samuel was conceived (1 Samuel Chapter 1).

So stay the course and pass the test, as your wait is not in vain because they that wait on the Lord shall renew their strength (Isaiah 40:31).

Stay strong in the Lord and don't lose heart.

The Father wants the very best for us and He is going to give you your best if you keep His commandments.

Psalm 37:4 says, "Delight yourself in the Lord, and he will give you the desires of your heart."

Let's pray.

Lord God, while I'm in my waiting season for my spouse, help me to focus on what you have for me to do in this season. Help me not to idolize what I see on social media and in the world. Help me to love myself the way you see me in every area of my life. In Jesus' name! Amen.

CHAPTER 5

Let the Father Lead You

Getting to know a person can be draining sometimes. I asked myself, "Why do we need to keep conducting interviews?" Why not? We have to make sure they align with the purpose that God has assigned to our lives. Everyone you meet is not for you and I had to learn that for myself. The enemy knows your desires and wants as well.

1 Peter 5:8 says, "Be sober-minded. Be alert. Your adversary, the devil, is prowling around like a roaring lion, looking for anyone he can devour." The devil's main purpose is to stop the purpose that the Lord has placed inside of you. When we move with the wrong person, we cause a delay in our own life. We get so caught up with what we see on social media or even television at times wanting what we see, but we have to remind ourselves to guard our ear/eye gates (Proverbs 4:20-22). There is an old saying that everything that glitter is not gold because it's not. Remember, we are in a day and age where people are all caught up in creating content for likes and views, not truth.

I would rather be alone than in a relationship where I'm still by myself. I've been there and never wanted to experience that again. Be with someone who treats you like the King or Queen that you are. Be with someone that brings peace and value to your life. Our God wants the very best for us, so if we give Him our will for His will and let Him guide us in these dating streets, we will be able to discern the counterfeit. In this season, where I have totally given my heart to the Lord, loneliness doesn't sneak in like it used to because my mind is always set on fulfilling God's purpose in my life.

If the Lord God has spoken to you that you will be a wife or husband, hold on to that prom-

ise and don't let go of it as His promises are yes and amen (2 Corinthians 1:20).

Let's Pray.

Lord God, guide my thoughts and my speech. Help me to make decisions with you included. If they're not of you, I don't want them, as you are the God of order and not confusion. I'm your child and you know what's best for me. Give me the spirit of discernment when I meet new people. I want your will and not mine.

In Jesus' name! Amen.

JOURNAL

Write down your deepest thoughts and desires on this page and place them at the feet of Jesus and believe it is done.

_____

_____

_____

_____

_____

Let the Father Lead You

The Waiting Season

CHAPTER 6

Enjoy The Years Of Your Singleness

I REMEMBER A TIME WHEN I had no problem getting a man (laughing hard in my head)! I still hear my cousin saying, "Do what you did back in the day when you always had a man." I'm saying to myself, "I didn't really do anything to get one in my younger years; they just came." I enjoyed the attention I would get from guys, but realized later why they flocked to me. I was a fixer. I would try to fix them up and pray that they would be what I needed them to be, but that left me broken.

After a while, I would start to question myself. I would say to myself, "Why am I not married? I should have kids and a pet by now." I would hear family say, "You got a man yet? Why do you not have a man? What are you doing and what did you do?" Is this a generational curse of why I'm still single? In turn, I questioned myself, "Why am I still single?" I got tired of hearing that over and over. After a while, I would try to force relationships or situationships so that I could be in a relationship. I looked for companionship in all the wrong places which left me empty inside.

I would do things to occupy my time to fill up my loneliness or make you know "that call I'm talking about" to fill that void. Eventually, I stopped because I was still feeling empty. There were times when I heard the Lord say, "Don't do it (because I wrote it in my journey)" and I still did it anyway. I did this off and on with the Lord until 2022. Life happened and I lost the only father I knew from the age of two. My dad's passing struck a chord in my spirit and I knew I could no longer live the way I was living. I was angry at myself for the mistakes I made over and over. I knew the Lord never left me, but I only gave Him pieces of me.

Can I be honest? I was so broken on the inside because my desires weren't met. At the time, I felt like I was doing everything right, but I wasn't. I was living a sinful life. I would repent, ask God for forgiveness, and go back and do it again. Yep, I was going to church and active in a lot of ministries, but still out of the will of God. Most people don't like to talk about that, but it's what makes us feel good for the moment. I no longer wanted a temporary fix. I wanted an eternal fix.

[19] Now the practices of the [a]sinful nature are clearly evident: they are sexual immorality, impurity, sensuality (total irresponsibility, lack of self-control), [20] [b]idolatry, [c]sorcery, hostility, strife, jealousy, fits of anger, disputes, dissensions, factions [that promote heresies], [21] envy, drunkenness, riotous behavior, and other things like these. I warn you beforehand, just as I did previously, that those who practice such things will not inherit the kingdom of God. [22] But the fruit of the Spirit [the result of His presence within us] is love [unselfish

concern for others], joy, [inner] peace, patience [not the ability to wait, but how we act while waiting], kindness, goodness, faithfulness, ²³ gentleness, self-control. Against such things there is no law. ²⁴ And those who belong to Christ Jesus have crucified the [d]sinful nature together with its passions and appetites. Galatians 5:19-24(AMP)

We have to learn to put our flesh under subjection daily, sometimes hourly, especially when we know what hinders us. The devil knows our weakness, so we have to identify what's of the Lord and what's of the enemy.

Enjoy this beautiful season that's before you. I have found that laying at Jesus' feet and spending alone time with him has been so rewarding. There is a newfound peace I have even when chaos is going on that comes from Him. There's something about when you draw closer to Him, He draws back to you (James 4:8). It's a feeling I get sometimes that's hard for me to explain to where I just sit and bask in His presence.

During this season, read the Bible, pray, go to church and conferences that build your faith, go on trips, enjoy brunches or dinner, find something that makes you happy. Don't get lost in your current situation. Enjoy what's in front. Remember, it's just a part of your WAITING SEASON.

Let's pray.

Dear Heavenly Father, Thank you for this season of singleness that you have placed before me. Just because I'm single doesn't mean I can't enjoy my life. Help me not focus on other relationships because when it's my turn, I know that the wait will be worth it. Thank you, Lord Jesus, for life that is satisfying with you. In Jesus' name! Amen.

JOURNAL

1. What are ways you can find joy in your singleness?
2. Write them down and once you finish that task, trip, etc., check it off and prepare yourself for your spouse.

_____

_____

The Waiting Season

Enjoy The Years Of Your Singleness

The Waiting Season

About The Author

Queenie Patton is a woman of God who absolutely loves people. Her family and friends will tell you that she doesn't meet a stranger. She loves inspiring and encouraging people through their journey in life and reminding them to live life on purpose.

Queenie has been an active member of the church since she was able to walk. The gifts she operates in are singing, praise dance, working with youth, and outreach ministry. Queenie is also very active in her community. She lives off of these scriptures: Proverbs 3:5-6, "Trust in the Lord with all your heart and lean not into your own understanding; In all your ways acknowledge him and he will direct your path." He will guide you in any area of your life if you surrender it to Him to guide you.

www.ingramcontent.com/pod-product-compliance
Lightning Source LLC
LaVergne TN
LVHW012049070526
838201LV00082B/3871